ABOUT THE AUTHOR

Kevin P. Gilday is an award-winning poet, writer and performer from Glasgow. He is the founder of poetry collective The Scribbler's Union and was co-founder of spoken word cabaret night Sonnet Youth. He is a National Theatre of Scotland Breakthrough Writer, a BBC Writersroom Scottish Voice and one of Scotland's most celebrated contemporary poets.

www.kevinpgilday.com

‘If you've ever wandered, bewildered, through a world of high rents, sticky romantic encounters, dying relationships and occasional, soaring triumphs then Kevin Gilday's Anxiety Music will speak to your soul. Fearless, hilarious and steeped in a Weegie-ness that still, somehow, manages to feel universal, this is poetry for our times. Gilday has turned self-doubt into an artform and brutal self-criticism into a relentless desire to communicate and find meaning in other people. It also contains the funniest sequence of sex poetry you will ever encounter in your life. Anxiety Music is the new soundtrack for your solipsism.’ - Alan Bissett

‘An accomplished purveyor of saline wit. Anxiety Music holds a mirror to the cult of individualism, surveying the wreckage with glimmers of hope and hard truths.’
- Victoria McNulty

‘A peerless poet and performer.’ - Darren McGarvey

‘You will have thought these thoughts before. Kevin has just articulated them for you.’ - Mike Garry

‘Anxiety music takes the grim and gritty parts of contemporary existence and turns it into something glorious. A confronting, comforting and captivating written soundtrack to modern life. From cunnilingus to capitalism, from drinking to divorce - the sharply witty interrogation of human joy and tragedy touches you in unexpected ways. Wouldn’t expect anything less from this leading voice in the Scottish spoken word scene. Tender and tough in all the right places’
- Cat Hepburn

‘This collection is life itself. Kevin's poems have an awe-inspiring ability to floodlight the world's ills whilst feeling like an afternoon in your favourite boozer. A stunning book.’ - Matt Abbott

'A wonderful collection written with such flair and warmth. I loved it.'
- Hannah Lavery

Kevin P. Gilday
Anxiety Music

BIRMINGHAM

PUBLISHED BY VERVE POETRY PRESS
https://vervepoetrypress.com
mail@vervepoetrypress.com

FIRST PUBLISHED SEP 2022

Printed and bound in the UK
by ImprintDigital, Exeter

ISBN: 978-1-913917-14-2

Cover and chapter artwork by Stephen Morton

for all those who hear the music,
let it play

CONTENTS

PREFACE

Tune up the band...

In June of 2019 I was due to fly out to Montreal for two weeks of shows and readings. In the days leading up to the trip I did all the usual things – sorting travel insurance, changing currency, packing bags, etc. – but as I got closer to the date a sense of dread started to grow in me. An anxiety, the type of which I'd never experienced, started to take me over. It was all consuming, a massive worry that blacked out everything else. I cancelled my trip and stayed in bed for weeks thinking about all the ways the world was going to end and all the terrible things that would happen to me for existing in it.

The Anxiety Music started to play.

This was the starting point for the collection. The anxiety that had manifested in my life was aching to be expressed. Since then I have been unpicking the threads of this breakdown, tracing back the outcome to the root causes. This anxiety did not appear fully formed from the ether, it had been slowly emerging from the recesses of my brain since I was a child. But was I the only one? I started to wonder how many other people felt like this, if the strangers I passed in the street were experiencing the swell of this same nameless dread.

Were we all tuned to the same anxious frequency?

I created this collection to express my discontent the only way I know how – through poetry – but also as an invitation. A chance to dive into these dark abysses together. To shine a light on their machinations with humour and compassion. Because I'm not the only passenger on this sinking ship, not the only citizen of this spiralling society – the apprehension we feel can either scare us into isolation or it can unite us in our shared humanity.

The collection is split into five sections, each reflecting a source of anxiety in our personal and collective existence: Modern Life, Capitalism, Sex, Memory and Loss.

All the good stuff.

The Only Constant is Chaos deals with the overwhelming sensation of just being alive in all this... From cancellation to Covid, nuclear war to climate change – it details the terrifying what ifs that keep us awake at night. The unshakeable angst of right now. Our restless birthright.

Late Capitalism Doesn't Want Me For a Sunbeam deals with the stress of existing in our unequal and damaging system. Poems that try to make some sense of a senseless construct, that attempt to pinpoint the individual in the crush of numbers that dictate our life, that memorialise this slow gentrification of the soul. These are poems that locate vital humanity in our unfair world, the hopeful kindling of revolution.

Ten Short Poems About Shagging is about... well, it's poems about shagging. But more explicitly about sexuality and repression. About the commodification of sex and the marketing of our pleasure. About how we hold back who we are at our own detriment.

All That Fucking Sand collects poems on loss and memory. Half remembered details from years ago that glitter in the torchlight, affording new insights when revisited. Thoughts about who we are, where we came from and if we can ever escape the path laid out for us. These are pieces that dig into our past in search of our future.

And finally, *On Leaving the Scene of the Crime* – poems about the break-up of a marriage. These pieces lay bare the stark reality of the end of a relationship. The unvarnished uncoupling of two lives and the mountains of teeming baggage that must be sorted in its wake.

Each could be the main theme of a collection in its own right, but – for me – the relationship between these concepts draws a picture of our troubled modern lives and our need for connection. Each poem is a jigsaw piece that when completed I hope will reveal both the portrait of a life and a mirror for the reader.

This collection deliberately bridges page and stage, encompasses craft and performance. It takes the doubtless electricity of live spoken word and captures it in passionate ink. It's an unfiltered look at the sources of anxiety that hi-jacked my life and my personal journey to confront them, but in doing so it's a statement of intent regarding what we will and what we will no longer accept from our short time on this earth. A rallying call to face the forces of anxiety wrought upon us by an uncaring society and fight back.

—Kevin P. Gilday, June 2022

Anxiety Music

THE ONLY CONSTANT IS CHAOS

In The Future Everyone Will Be Cancelled for 15 Minutes

The purity test must be passed
Your history ransacked for muck
Context is relative
If you simply don't give a fuck
Your fave is problematic
And so is your love
Look, I don't make the rules ok?
They're decreed from above
Your mask slipped once
Now you've forfeited your humanity
And there's a digital mob at the door
Testing the edges of your sanity
The rules of engagement
Pushed to their limits
In the future
Everyone will be cancelled for 15 minutes

Nuance is cancelled
Forgiveness is cancelled
Perspective is cancelled
Yer auld da is cancelled
Listening is cancelled
Understanding is cancelled
Debate is cancelled
This Scotrail service is cancelled

Perfection attained through fear
Here's the line, stick to it
Say it aloud, then toe it
Repeat it like a holy writ
Expectations have been set
At a frankly unachievable height
Still, failure will not be tolerated
When we've outlined what is right
Though the memo was internal
And never distributed widely
It's up to you to stay informed
And to regurgitate blindly
Feel the warm glow of superiority
Let it lift your waning spirits
In the future
Everyone will be cancelled for 15 minutes

Subtlety is cancelled
Respect is cancelled
Dissent is cancelled
Your shitty poetry is cancelled
Opinion is cancelled
Opposition is cancelled
Deviation is cancelled
Your existence is cancelled

And I'm so scared I'll get it wrong
Rouse a skeleton to emerge walking
From the dark recesses of my wardrobe
Let the past do all the talking
And there won't be any defence
Because a bluebird doesn't listen

Just a public defenestration
And an unyielding presupposition
But I am part of the problem
Preach understanding while holding the whip
Hope others' misdemeanours will deflect
As I maintain my tenuous grip
We need patience in place of exile
Change powered by the love within it
Or in the future
Everyone will be cancelled for 15 minutes

After The Flood

I eat my toast as they count the dead
Suppress a ripple of abstract grief
With every obnoxious tick
Of the metronomic counter
Held hostage by aquatic anxiety

The flood came suddenly
A primal fury untethered from the sky
It ripped across the globe like dusk
A pestilence passed from latitude to longitude

We observed the water levels rise
With ethnological pleasure
Dispassionately noted the details
As it enveloped the famous streets of ancient cities
Pointing to the clavicles of the great buildings
We had gazed upon, ten summers hence
A polaroid recollection
Stripped to skeleton

But it was still not enough for us
To accept the forthcoming reality
Dismissed as foreign language feature
When it was instead a trailer
Coming soon to a country near you...

We saw soon enough
It didn't take long to make landfall
From abstruse concept to brutal verity
A tide of panic
Uncontrollable
Unmistakable
Unprecedented

Now we live in thrall of the flood
Inhabit the icy folds
Pull the surf around us like a blanket
My flat is filled with it
My clothes are damp from it
I ship it out in buckets
But it returns to me
A persistent drip drip drip of dread
And so I learn to live in the water
Go about my day in the deep end
I eat my toast as they count the dead

After the flood
There will be an armada of bodies
Washed upon the shore
Evidence of when the levee broke
And the Clyde burst its banks
Overflowing with the forgotten fathers
Of abandoned care homes

After the flood
The guillotines will be sharpened
With the cursed names
Of every politician who pontificated
While the lists lengthened
Of every billionaire who burnished
Their bulging bank account
Of every deviant who denied it
Hid behind piles of privilege
As their neighbours drowned

After the flood
We will rebuild the bridges of humanity
In simple sustainability
Live within the everyday alchemy of being
Treat the tenets of our home like a temple

After the flood
We will ring bells across this land
In triumph and in mourning
A wake-up call to humanity
A harbinger of the fight to come
We will lay out the corpses as a border
For our brave new world
Recite their names as a battle hymn

Grateful for our shelter when the storm came
And forever mindful
Of the eventual cascade that will one day
Sweep us all away

Mediocre White Man Blues

I hear them like a military choir
Singing a Stereophonics chorus
An army of stale pasty men
Put on this earth to bore us
Old Spice as the chosen scent
Dick pics as pick-up lines
Even Stevie fucking Wonder
Could read the warning signs
Stinking of desperation, reeking of booze
I've got the mediocre white man blues

I've got the mediocre white man blues
I've got the mediocre white man blues
It's up to me to pick and choose
I've got the mediocre white man blues

There's a wanky student at the party
Not embarrassed to show it
The poor fucker's read Bukowski
And he wants you to know it
Starts quoting lines of Joyce
Like he's the first cunt ever reading him
If he starts on the Dostoevsky
I'm sticking the fucking heid in him
A conversational turning of the screws
I've got the mediocre white man blues

I've got the mediocre white man blues
I've got the mediocre white man blues
Don't gotta read no social cues
I've got the mediocre white man blues

Dissecting five-a-sides
Like it's the World Cup Final
I much prefer their earlier stuff
And it sounds better on vinyl
Tell us about your fitness regime
So unrelentingly grim
Who needs a personality
When you've got the gym
Ten inch biceps, size five shoes
I've got the mediocre white man blues

I've got the mediocre white man blues
I've got the mediocre white man blues
No need to hide my problematic views
I've got the mediocre white man blues

You can't say anything nowadays
You tweet to your ten followers
No irony to be spared
Amongst your clan of keyboard warriors
This isn't a free speech issue
There's no overflowing queue
You've not been deplatformed
Just no cunt wants to book you
Who let this wank on the ten o'clock news?
I've got the mediocre white man blues

I've got the mediocre white man blues
I've got the mediocre white man blues
Picked Ayn Rand as my hipster muse
Now I've got the mediocre white man blues

All the opportunity that was promised
Has been stolen from me
Served up silver platter style
With a diverse snowflake decree
The future I was entitled to
Has been taken by those that want it
My story is old, been told
Shoved down throats 'til we vomit
Maybe I need to admit I'm responsible for this spew
Because I'm a mediocre white man too

I've got the mediocre white man blues
I've got the mediocre white man blues
Nothing left to learn, nothing left to lose
I've got the mediocre white man blues

Bastards

Critically acclaimed bastards
Award-winning bastards
Wunderkind bastards
Authentic, working class bastards
Connected, middle class bastards
Previously published with... bastards
Longlisted bastards
Shortlisted bastards
Forward Prize bastards
Week-long residential bastards
Glastonbury bastards
Fringe bastards
Just-found-my-calling bastards
Just-stumbled-in bastards
Urban bastards
Rural bastards
Pretending to be bohemian, learned a bit of French bastards
5 lines arranged randomly on Instagram bastards
Ignorant bastards
Ungrateful bastards
Shameless bastards

Bastards
Bastards
Bastards

Anxiety Music

Wherever I go
I hear it
The anxiety music

The unfinished symphony
The merciless drone
The atonal attack
The incessant pop chorus
The anxiety music

My neurological dials, tilted
Tuned in
To the rhythm of a raised heartbeat
A weary waltz of what-ifs
Can you hear it?

It's there in the supermarket queue
Rehearsing your only line
Like a third-rate actor
Translating a bus ticket
To inky pulp

It's there in the pre-flight announcement
Tracing the pilot's voice for a hint of doubt
A polygraph of panic
Angered by your blatant disregard
For the wonders of gravity

Lately, *the anxiety music* has grown louder
Heralded by fascistic trumpets
Amplified by the unrelenting buzz of the internet
I hear it in the dark cubicle of my subconscious
Composing a lopsided poem to ego
A 4am, 130BPM
Techno trauma, jangling
My nervous sound system

On a Sunday evening
Just as the sun sets
The anxiety music seems to seep
From every wall
And I am a child again
It's the ice level from Mario Brothers 3
And my dad singing Deacon Blue
And an ashtray of fags
Burning themselves out of existence

The anxiety music sometimes sounds
Like a symphony of misfiring bus engines
Backed by a choir
Of well-meaning
Constructive criticism
The brass phasing an apocalyptic scale
Scoring a thousand painful deaths
All the ways the music will end

And when it does
When the record scratches and skips
Will we wonder if we conceived all that disquiet
As a smokescreen to mask our failure
Against all that perceived danger
Robbing us of our chance to live fully
To enjoy our footloose three chords
And marvel at our glorious middle eight
Before everything we know
Turns to static

Ring Light

Am I an ugly bastard? Am I an ugly bastard? Am I an ugly bastard? Am I an ugly bastard? Am I an ugly bastard? Am I an ugly bastard? Am I an ugly bastard? Am I an ugly bastard? Am I an ugly bastard?

Am
I
An
Ugly
Bastard?

Personal Best

On Sundays
I lace up sky-blue trainers
And attempt to outrun my anxiety
I race ennui around the city
As the weekend's dregs are drunk
By those who do not want it to end

I carry a week of trouble
In my underdeveloped muscles
Thursday's quiet drinks
Became Saturday's session
And suddenly,
Sunday
Is a lonely place
An ellipsis at the end of my week
With a nagging question that asks
How many do I have left?

An app informs me
I have run very far indeed
And passed many fellow
Lycra-clad apparitions
On my destination-less journey
Fluorescent wraiths
Drifting across the spare ground
Searching for life in the downtown lights

There is the illusion of freedom here
A placebo of control
I decide what streets to melodically beat
With the free jazz strokes of my feet
How fast the landscape moves
Curling around me like a zoetrope
I am the master of my destiny -
Until my legs begin to fail me

And reward is earned
An hour-long high
Aroused into being
By a heady translation of chemicals
Mixing and mingling in my brain
Like a cheap cocktail

And the comedown is inevitable
That potent potion disassembling itself
One pleasure-loving molecule at a time
Leaving me to contemplate,
With cruel clarity,
The unyielding loneliness of existence
In the dark

On nights like this
The city cocoons itself
In an autumnal glaze
Air filled with damp smoke
And half-lit graffiti
On crumbling walls
The esoteric messages
Of apprentice gangsters

Now grown up
Selling insurance in calls centres
And lacing up sky-blue trainers
On a Sunday

The Only Constant is Chaos

The only constant is chaos
The heavy hands of history mould
From Glasgow City to Lagos
Equilibrium is a lie we're sold

The heavy hands of history mould
Wars that break peace like a dreadnought
Equilibrium is a lie we're sold
Illusion shattered with the sound of a gunshot

Wars that break peace like a dreadnought
Fumes that melt ice like a desert
Illusion shattered with the sound of a gunshot
Or the mortal-grim findings of the expert

Fumes that melt ice like a desert
From Glasgow city to Lagos
Or the mortal-grim findings of the expert
The only constant is chaos

(Also, Love)

Love insists on reaching out a hand   needy
Threatening to pull me   from quagmire
Or pit   an eternal presence/annoyance

To learn   to trust
To read   the signs
To train   for help
Is our masterpiece   unfinished

Relationships shift   tectonic
Split the landscape   in two
But always   love is waiting
At a new location   we first need
To tune   to melodious signal
Travel to greet it   at some temporary home

Love returns   like a season
Punchdrunk pugilist   coming back for more
Pristine towel   left seething on rail

Love still insists   after all this
Keeps reaching out   a haggard hand
Asks only   that we meet it
Half way

Tipping Point

The horizon is fixed with a pin
That holds back history
The inconceivable future
Becomes the pregnant present
Birthed from the pages
Of torn sci-fi novels
Into a turbulent now

And here we are at the tipping point
The ripping point
The on-a-jolly-whisky-sipping point
A point of order
A point of contention
A point of no return

It is one minute to midnight
And still the debate continues
Voices negotiate their duty
Attempt to shirk responsibility
Excuses unspooled like a net
Designed to displace obligation
In its wide-eyed weaving

Even as the tipping point looms into focus
Reveals itself as cliff edge
We talk of time
Hold the future like a concept
Data to be shaped and reviewed
Sculpted by the current

But who will we blame
When the theoretical manifests
Our failure written
In charred remains

Here at the tipping point
The tripping point
The can't-you-feel-it-just-slipping point
The moment of truth
The moment of action
The moment of change

I am tired of being carried
On the broken back of zeitgeist
My agency reduced to sorting cardboard
Playing with plastic
While glacial policy protects
The profit of those responsible -
A nihilist's dream

The tipping point
The gripping point
The last-vestiges-of-hope-stripping point
The time is now
The time is running out
The time has already passed

We are at the tipping point
Regarding oblivion below
And we know, doubtless
Only our collective weight
Can redress the balance

but by then

we had forgotten the word for Butterfly.
So long had a human stamped
an imperious eye
on a tracing paper wing.

No nonagenarian description
could flutter justice
to their something colour
or something something form.

Consigned to the forgotten
pages of buried books.
Their beauty now
unimaginable.

Will there at least be time for a retrospective?

I need the world to exist
Just long enough
To declare me, a genius
Revisit those overlooked masterpieces
Pamper me with posthumous validation
A serious re-evaluation
I need a scholar to find the thematic link
Between my second collection
And my fourth album
Provide what I was never afforded in life

I want:
Goths to scratch my lines into notebooks
Teenagers to fuck on my gravestone
A retrospective full of beard-stroking wankers
Tugging themselves to ecstasy
Over the inherent themes
And thinly veiled subtexts
In my decomposing body of work

But, I worry

I worry
That future generations will read these words
And my woes will feel so small to them
Look at this old poet!
Lamenting his career

As he was living like a king
In the last days of Rome
Condemning us to the bleakness
Of an unforgivable future

He created art while the world burned
Talked of himself incessantly
And engaged with his era's hate
In only the most performative of ways
Like this was all for him –

A film set for some small-scale drama
A brief blink of an existence
While the earth heated around him
Slow as an oven
The real narrative unfolding
While he attempted to conjure some meaning
In the spaces between the words

And when the end *inevitably* comes
Collect the detritus my ambition left behind –
The Lidl bags of poems
The books, the CDs, the records
The piles of scripts spoken by actors
Long since departed
That one novel that no-one ever published –
And dump them in a wheelbarrow
Push it to the top of the highest hill
Just as the water begins to rise

And read
Read all my words aloud
And hear me
Hear all my stunted attempts at connection
All the times I tried to share a little of me
With you
The ideas that brought me joy
And all the things that scared me

Give me my retrospective, finally
At the top of a hill
At the end of the world

And when the sun sets that final time
You do what you must
Set fire to the remnants of my life
And sit for a few minutes
In the silence
Appreciating the simple pleasure
Of a warm goodbye

LATE CAPITALISM
DOESN'T WANT ME
FOR A SUNBEAM

In A Dublin Pisser

In a Dublin pisser
I relieve myself of a €6 Heineken
Wearing the porcelain smooth
With a history of spirits
An interweaving tapestry
Of pish
In this riverside hostelry turned
Tacky museum of plastic paddy past
I think of the rough men who once did the same
The dockers, the porters, the factory workers
How they would fill this cramped room with laughter
Turn the air blue on the fine tip of a filthy joke
And I wonder, what they'd think of me

In a Dublin pisser
My bladder conjures a river
As I recall my maiden voyage
To these ancient shores
Sure my name would be a passport
Trigger a long-planned celebration
A riotous homecoming
Of tricolour tickertape
Before discovering
With amber disappointment
That I was just another homesick tourist
Weary with modernity
Groping around for an identity
In the hollows of the past
Wallet open to any amateur historian

Who could bestow some meaning
On a sad wee boy from Glasgow
Who grew up listening
To too many Wolfetones records

In a Dublin pisser
I dream a meandering future in this city
All literary clichés
And adopted phraseology
My harsh vowels embraced in a Celtic knot
A second chapter of overdue respect
But the artists moved out
When the money moved in
Gentrification as cultural cleansing
It's fucking deadly right enough, lads
When London is a viable alternative
Killing off the saplings of creativity
Filling in the fertile ground of community
With boxes of impenetrable concrete
And glass shrines to the malevolent gods of capital

In a Dublin pisser
The seal is broken,
So are the tiles
And I wonder -
Like the fucking idiot I am -
If Joyce or Beckett or Heaney
Ever held their shrivelled cock at this urinal
Letting the liquid inspiration flow
And what they'd think of the old place now
All Airbnb lodgers
Transient ghosts holding four leaf clovers

En route to the Guinness Storehouse
Streets overlaid with the double negative
Of a 1916 theme park
To which I have purchased the full package
Novelty photograph and all

I let the recycled air
Dry the European water from my hands
And breathe in my counterfeit birthright
Liffey smog, unfiltered
Patron saint of borrowed nostalgia
For all of us who trace our lines across oceans
Taking the journey of our ancestors in reverse
Trying to understand their hardship
As we fly unmolested across the Irish sea
The snakes returning home
Quicker than it takes a pint to settle

The Old Men In Wetherspoons Are Angry About The Politics

A Union Jack flops flaccidly
Heralding the best of British ales
The sterile silence broken only by the rustle of a tabloid
Sun, Star, Mail
A bedraggled buffet of a breakfast club
Reserved for the dedicated morning shift
Pints are sipped while lines are reviewed
Studiously ignoring the stench of pish

The old men in Wetherspoons are angry about the politics
Another migrant boat, another pointless vote
Not that anyone thought to ask them
They may as well be ghosts
Used to work every day
Trade sweat for respect, a modest cheque
But those days are gone
Left with two dodgy knees and a crick in the neck

And this theme park pub harks back
A reconstruction of an ideal
Distorted through golden arch economics
Pints served with a fast food feel
But it's open early for business
And everyone keeps to themselves
The telly is tuned to Sky Sports News
As the atmosphere compels

This is it
Born to shit
A plastic
Scrapheap of
Formless wit
We're exiled
And reviled
Jizzed on the
Fake leather
An unwan
-ted stepchild

The old men in Wetherspoons are angry about the politics
Worked all their days just to get fuck all
While the paper says some immigrant prick
Gets a free smartphone to call
Home, to whatever shithole country
He sailed to escape
All those years of paying taxes
Was surely a mistake

How can they fail to feel
That all power has been lost
When control doesn't reside in calloused hands
When ballot slips are crossed
So the pub becomes a dominion
A jurisdiction marked out in empties
Delineated by the 8-bit wail of the puggy machine
Devouring a wallet of crisp twenties

The old men in Wetherspoons are angry about the politics
Coached in their rage from every angle

Trained to be incensed at the latest scandal
What opinion is yours to disentangle?
When the papers scream blue murder
and the TV edits the truth
The algorithm recommends conspiracy theories
While the radio phone-in carries the proof

This is it
Born to shit
No trust for
You feckless
Hypocrites
We're exiled
And reviled
Ignored by
A cabal
Of wanton
Paedophiles

The old men in Wetherspoons are angry about the politics
And I find it hard to blame them
An army of amateur analysts
Lining up to shame them
Have you ever felt forgotten?
Like the world has left you behind?
Thursday night means curry club
Debit card declined

Said

The letting agent said
A wisny rich enough tae stay here

The hoosing association said
A wisny poor enough tae stay there

The mortgage lender said
They canny help me oot
No wae that joab

The big beautiful world said
Ye're no comin oor here
(no wae that joab)

Ma Da said
A've tae get ma life sorted oot

Ma ex said
Well, this is wit ye wanted
Wis it no?

Ma pal said
See, the problem wae you
Is ye're never fucking satisfied

And aye,
Ah suppose they'd aw be right
With wit they

Late Capitalism Doesn't Want Me for a Sunbeam

My light shines for me alone
It is not a commodity
An anonymous outlier
Who refuses to participate
Offering its limp body up
With the blunt blade of necessity
My worth cannot be tied
In a system that ignores me

Murdering my time

Why am I so desperate to succeed?

When the world turns on greed

I am useless to the cause

In the daily sacrifice

At the crooked feet of capital

To my place in society

To be packaged and sold

The Free Market Stole My Humanity (And I Want It Fucking Back)

This poem is a bomb
Not a metaphorical one
An. Actual. Fucking. Bomb.
A searing Molotov cocktail
Of language and discontent
My blistering anger, the righteous accelerant
That will ignite my syntax
And singe that single stray, grey hair
On your middle class
Eyebrows

This poem is a protest song
Chanted through the letterbox
Of your semi-detached
An implacable cacophony of resistance
Beaten into brilliant existence
On my Grannie's pots and pans
A syncopated rhythm of generational poverty
Deposited in the ivory towers
Of your inner cochlea
Like a mail-order wine club

This poem is a battered minibus
Chartered to pick up your wayward children
From their ten-grand-a-year private school
But I have rerouted the satnav
Retuned the Radio 1 caterwaul

And replaced it
With the complete works of Billy Bragg
Plied your sheltered offspring
With ten times the recommended daily allowance
Of refined sugar
(which is the worst kind)
And set them loose to make new friends
In a multicultural neighbourhood -
Blazerless

This poem is a sledgehammer
A truculent tool
Embedded in the windscreen of your BMW
Like a sundial
Designed to destroy
The collective front door
Of every crummy, buy-to-let landlord
Currently lining their pockets with our labour
Your sinuous end of tenancy itinerary
Will record my metaphors squatting
In the dark recesses of the hall cupboard
A permanent resident
Until you address
The elephantine scandal
In the rented room

This poem is a party crasher
An uninvited drifter
Come to spill uncomfortable truths
On your good rug
And slip Bella Ciao
Into your carefully curated party playlist

Inflicting a pre-made powerpoint presentation
On any ignoramus
Who dares utter that they
Just don't do politics
It will piss in the close
Of unchecked capital
It will shit in the kettle
Of big business
And it will redistribute the fridgeful of cans
Equally

This poem is a mirror
An echo of my desires
Imprinted in coke-smeared reflection
It invokes a latent image
An animated tableau of an easy life
That makes my heart leap with lust
Pieces falling into place with simple grace
Like a children's jigsaw
But would I still be driven
To burn this system to the ground
If it benefited me?
Is my anger formed from injustice
Or just jealousy?

This poem is a love poem
Not a red, red rose
But an evergreen affection
For the unending resilience requisite
To improve the lot of a stranger
This is the passion required
To reshape the world

A blueprint sketched with a bookie's pen
On the reverse
Of this poem

My Landlord's Home

In my landlord's home there rests:

A serenely smiling Buddha statue,
Carved in sparkling jade, clasped hands askew.

A weighted record player of pinpoint fidelity,
Spinning Beatles reissues like an atrocity.

A mini fridge for Prosecco of exulted name,
Cava being not quite the same.

A seeping sense of chronic guilt,
Gagged by a privilege custom-built.

House plants that have chosen suicide.
A monolithic fridge-freezer fortified,

By munros of organic produce.
A hidden history of child abuse.

A working boiler of tectonic build,
Capable of lasting the winters chilled.

A framed print of unparalleled detail,
Affixed to the wall with a single nail.

Photos of beloved grandkids replete w/ beaming wife,
None of whom will want for a thing in this life.

Furniture not pulled bloody and loose,
From Ikea's cheapest gums like a prized tooth.

A millionaire's biography hastily typeset,
A guide to changing your underdeveloped mindset.

A feeling of dread, skulking and hungry,
That creeps in like a burglar every other Sunday.

cess (noun)

We have too much round here
An excess in these parts
More than our fair share
And enough to spare
Mortality

It seeps from our taps
A slow dancing poison
Climbs perilous out the window
Of the high flats
Scales the wall
Behind the butchers
Dives for fag doubts
Outside the shopping centre
A surplus of this mortality

This city breathes it in
A profusion of cessation
Particles plunged into the air
From ancient factory pipes
Laden with asbestos
An industrial nightmare
Oblivious to the winds of change

Down the road they have just enough
But here we are inundated
This 'Glasgow effect'
That turns beloved sons

To drug addict statistics
That strips a diet down
To tins and boxes
A glut of mortality

Your maw would always claim she didn't have a favourite. But it was definitely you. We could tell as she put you in the ground. Our dear green place, fertilised with the bodies of the forgotten. Your membership to that Tuesday morning Methadone crew. Nerves jangling, until one day they didn't.

And no-one can tell us why
Why we keep dying
Why there's a funeral parlour in every scheme
Why our wake outfits
Hang heavy with expectation
On the back of bedroom doors

So we learn to wallow in the waiting
Biding time til our turn
Scanning the *Evening Times* obituaries
Memorialising colleagues and classmates
Faces revealing themselves
From foggy memory
Like a brass rubbing

'Right enough, the big man wasn't looking too good last I saw him'

They don't seem to have an answer
As to why it resides here
Our ASBO neighbour
Aggressively lurking at the close door
Funny how this excess
Sits neatly in a postcode like a stray
And for the life of you
For the life of us
No-one can say why

And what should I say to the teenage mothers pushing firstborns in second hand prams? Babies fed on mould and spores. Expectancy stunted. A life interrupted, by this exorbitant mortality.

And I wait every day
For this invisible force
To add me to the graph
An outlier
Marking the trend
Beside family and friends
Our little crosses
Recorded on a whiteboard
A sociologist's nightmare

And I dispute the details
Of my mother's death certificate
That did not record poverty,
A lifetime of it,
As cause

But round here
They call it excess mortality
They call it inevitable
They call it life
If they had the courage
They would call it what it is –
They would call it
Genocide

Death Cult

Capitalism is a death cult
To which we're signed up at birth
Names entered into the system
Indoctrinated and cursed
With the burden of just being
Alive, in the indifferent churn
That will swallow us up the second
Our hamster wheels don't turn

{capitalismisadeathcultcapitalismis}

An infernal machine
With only one direction and gear
Straight forward into the abyss
Like a genocidal pioneer
The planet is ablaze
Cooked by unsustainable growth
Fed valiantly by the flames
Of our suicidal oath

*{capitalismisadeathcultcapitalismisadeathcultcapitali
smisadeathcultcapitalismisadeathcultcapitalismisa
death}*

Hear the gnashing jaws,
Grind and wail
Feel the sharpened spears,
Primed to impale
Witness the daily evidence,

Consequences if you fail
And try...
To have a productive day

*{Capitalismisadeathcultcapitalismisadeathcultcapitalism
isadeathcultcapitalismisadeathcultcapitalismisadeathcult
capitalismisadeathcultcapitalismisadeathcult}*

Capitalism is a death cult
A dark religion sweeping the globe
Demanding its atomised denizens
Assume the position and disrobe
A chilling manifesto
Of unrepentant greed
Where to trample is to protect
And to survive is to succeed

*(Capitalismisadeathcultcapitalismisadeathcultcapitalism
isadeathcultcapitalismisadeathcultcapitalismisadeathcult
capitalismisadeathcultcapitalismisadeathcultcapitalismis
adeathcultcapitalismisadeathcultcapitalismis}*

The final bell of the old ways
The death rattle of avarice
Parade the billionaires through the streets
Cold and cadaverous
The disenfranchised of this world
Refuse to be ritual sacrifice
Our value as human beings
No longer tied to our market price

*{Capitalismisadeathcultcapitalismisadeathcultcapitalism
isadeathcultcapitalismisadeathcultcapitalismisadeathcult
capitalismisadeathcultcapitalismisadeathcultcapitalism
isadeathcultcapitalismisadeathcultcapitalismisadeath
capitalismisadeathcultcapitalismisadeath}*

Hear the gnashing jaws,
Grind and wail
Feel the sharpened spears,
Primed to impale
Witness the daily evidence,
Consequences if you fail
And try...
To have a productive day

*{Capitalismisadeathcultcapitalismisadeathcultcapitalism
isadeathcultcapitalismisadeathcultcapitalismisadeathcult
capitalismisadeathcultcapitalismisadeathcultcapitalismis
adeathcultcapitalismisadeathcultcapitalismisadeathcapitalism
isadeathcultcapitalismisadeathcultcapitalismisadeathcult
capitalismisadeathcultcapitalismisadeathcult}*

Scottish Psycho

I dream of discounted sofas
And smile a Mona Lisa
Vividly imagining the cool relief
Of a compliment
On my unexpected style

The algorithm has its claws in me
Adverts of my interior fantasies
Assault my periphery
Like an errant Rorschach
Of my deepest desires

I project my new home as an ideal
A parlour for intellectuals
A kitchen for gourmet
A bed for orgies
There is perfection to be attained
In the coordination of colour schemes
Matching rich tones
With earthy hues
Peace in our time

I dream of writing a masterpiece
On a desk of reclaimed wood
Birthing a work of genius
Triggering a celebratory soirée
Descending into a debauched bacchanalia
Of excessive praise

There's something in all of this
Domestic bliss
A nesting principle
Primal in origin
I should have out-evolved
But here I am
Listening intently to the chimp inside me
When he demands
An art deco drinks cabinet
(For some reason)

I thought I floated above
The uncouth stream of material want
Immune to the crude psychology
Of targeted ads and seasonal sales
But I cracked like a Fabergé egg
Within second sight
Of a vintage telephone seat

I used to travel the world
Marching across stages
Like a foreign invader
Home was a tenuous concept
A base for adventures
And where I slept became sacred
For the duration

Now I dream of surfaces
Perfectly varnished
And the world coming to me
Friends lined up around the block
To marvel at my interior design prowess
While I wait patiently to die

Cannibal City

1.
You only live as long
As the last person to remember you

I'm already forgetting your streets

2.
This is a cannibal city
It eats itself daily
The monuments of my childhood
Now recycled
Chopped up for parts
Reconstructed into something profitable

They saved the antiquity of wealth
The ornate halls of the merchants
Iced with marble
Gilded with gold
While the art deco brilliance
Of the cinemas and music halls
Was sold off cheap
The cultural history of the working classes
Bulldozed without opinion

If we don't remember the best of us
Then what chance for the rest of us?
When rooms that once roared with laugher
And reverberated with applause
Are lost to the whims of developers

Deaf to the echoing encores
Blind to the value of joy

While the names stay the same
A roll call of slavers and plantation owners
Buchanan, Glassford, Virginia, Jamaica
Let this past we have buried
In the name of progress
Come home to roost in our hearts

3.
A personal tour of the places that made me:

Do you not know that I got a handjob
In the backseat of that cinema?
A soft-focus Odeon fumble
Now an office for serious, suited young men

Do you not know that this stark shell
Used to be a Littlewoods?
Where my mum stoically scanned shopping
While I stowed away inside her

Are you not aware
That on the site of these new-build atrocities
There once stood a pub of real character?
Where my dad sat me down with a can of cola
While the real drinking got done

That the very place I was born is now a garden?
A memory of a generation
Who took their first breath
Within a few magical square feet

4.
And the cafes become coffee shops
And the bars become bistros
And the traders become Tescos
And we no longer know where we are

5.
But am I asking too much?
Do I want to wander in a wonderland of my own creation?
Clinging on to the familiar city I knew
Even as it evolves
Am I attempting to stop the world spinning?
Because the faster it goes, the more it changes
And the further I am from my youth

When the truth is
It is our actions that outlive us
Not the bricks we fashion into buildings
But our intention for doing so
And the houses I build of my love
Will shelter a few who will not long forget

You only live as long
As the last person to remember you
If that's true
I hope my name rings
Around the hollows of this old town
For years to come

Audition

He said:
I'm looking for a regional accent
Meaning, of course
Someone who sounds poor
But they can't put that in a voiceover casting call
Which is fair enough

Ah sed:
Pal, ahm regional as fuck
See, this is ma real voice
No the wan a use wae the likes ae you
It's heaving wae the auld p-o-v-e-r-t-y
Aw authentic an mistreatit an that

He said:
That's perfect, we'll let you know

Ah sed:
I'm looking forward to hearing from you

But a know ah never will
Cause ah wiz a touch too authentic
An naebody likes when hings git too real
Specially when ye're just trying
Tae sell a bit ae contents insurance

The Hungry Algorithm

A song rips ecstatic
Heavenly throb
Pure aural perfection
        Promoting no particular emotion

And as I dried the arteries of salt
On my now-glowing cheeks
I realised
I was redundant -
And so was the music
The hungry algorithm
Had swallowed us whole
        Made creation a myth

See, somewhere in the recent past
Choice became a burden
Our free time pressured into diamonds
Rare, priceless,
        To be outsourced

So, we began to trust
A benevolent intelligence
That would recommend us:
A song we might like
Or a t-shirt that would suit us
Or a new restaurant
        And it was *good*

We surrendered judgement to the machine
Liberating time, streamlining reality
Foregrounding efficiency
The only sacrifice was invisible
Our data mined like digital gold
(or more likely coal)
But what did that matter
When we clawed back a few minutes
    From the waning day?

The hungry algorithm hoovered up
Every crumb of content
The light dust cast from our essence
Shaped golems from our leftovers
    Until we could no longer tell the difference

Soon the entity was omnipresent
It decided:
Our job
Our address
Our lovers
    The future mapped out in statistics

Our personality a profile
Discovery pre-empted
My next obsession already decided
    Spontaneity usurped by convenience

And
  Art
    Was
      Dead

But some of us remember
The days before the music died
We recall the illicit thrill:
Of a crackling amp pushed too far
Of a drumkit primally pounded
        Of a lone voice connecting us in the dark

But these are tired tales now
Instead the hungry algorithm
Composes a noise, just for you
You do not need to share it
And no-one will ever know it
        A rare, mundane heaven

While in an oblivious corner
Of my functional dwelling
An old record player sits sternly
Turned down so as not to disturb
As I spin incorporeal voices
Into imperfect existence
Hear their words tease my cilia
Climb through an open window
Into a stranger's mind
        For just a few minutes

And then
And only then
Do I truly
        Feel alive

(Another) Death in Duke Street

After Edwin Morgan

The old greybeard, coffin dodger,
Boozebag extraordinaire
Breathed his proverbial
In phlegm-spitting distance
Of the artisan coffee dispensary
Without a single stray thought
For council mandates

Selfish bastard

He existed as a cautionary tale
An inconvenient relic
Of old Glasgow:
Territorial pissings on stair-affixed fixie bikes,
Spoiling the close Ping-Pong tourney
With a volley (and return) of abuse
His son waiting for him to snuff it
With pound signs in his eyes
And a photo of a Spanish villa
Carried in his wallet like a wish

They're dying off at a rate now
The old characters of Britain's longest street
The toy shop that electrified my youth
With its plastic aeroplane buzzing overhead
And the sawdust pubs
Of matchday sardines
Have all met their maker
Or estate agent

There are silent deaths
Almost every night
Local institutions fall
Revert to an empty chrysalis
Before they are renewed
Reborn one fine Dennistoun morning
As a shop for cacti
Distorting the established bookie lines
With a deep green, hand-painted signage
The prickly edge of progress

It starts as a rumble
A rumour of things to come
A sign announcing European funding
And the dawn of the future
Before the wave drives East
A tsunami of change
Funnelled along the Gallowgate
A stream of mixed-use modernisation
Mid-market Molendinar
From which we should all bend a knee
And sup gratefully

As the hungry ambulance
Casually swallows his limp body
Like an ethanol biscuit
A *FOR SALE* sign is already being erected
Beside the frost-bitten fairy lights
Of the communal herb garden

And every day
Flats are bought to rent
Taken from the community
And held hostage
Domestic extortion
Perpetrated by the aspirational
And the just plain selfish
Until each tenured resident
Is replaced by a transient student
Or wide-eyed young professional couple
Who would gladly barter blood
To call these claret bricks home
If only the price wasn't so high

TEN SHORT POEMS ABOUT SHAGGING

I Hope I Die At An Orgy

I hope I die at an orgy
Being pummelled by an accountant from Falkirk
Named Keith
On his day off from work
Fingering a Fiona
With my outstretched hand
As I attempt to breathe
Amongst the velvet folds
Of a generous woman
Whose name I did not catch
As we smiled across the buffet
Just a half an hour earlier

Armitage Shanks

To meet here,
to indulge our needs
where fetid fluids are jettisoned,
feels the very height
of council sleaze.

As you took me
tenderly between balmed lips
my eyes rolled back,
glimpsed electricity bathing
an idle synapse,
then wandered
to the familiar insignia
stamped above
your slowly nodding head

armitage shanks.
Transports me back
to austere school toilets.
Lingering around sinks,
leaking self-confidence,
reading the artless graffiti
of lurid deeds
I could only imagine
when god was not looking.

A wandering tongue
brings me back to the present

on a wave of euphoria.
I tempt a hand
through short, smooth hair
as you begin
to pick up the pace.

If only that shy boy
could see me now.

Gut

I know perceived wisdom
Would have me disgusted
But there's nothing
Quite as beautiful
As my gut
Resting gently
On your back

While yours ripples
With pleasure
A Mexican wave of expectation
With every thrust

I lay you river flat
And cascade my trunk
Across your rich curves
Like a landslip
Let you feel the weight
Of me
Unashamedly present

Necropolis

A classic summer day stretched out
Like the ubiquitous cat in the sun
As we slalomed between the graves
Of the dearly departed
Their names and dates eroding
Even stone unable
To hold their history intact

We took the shade of a tree
Without asking
And immediately got on with the task
Of getting off:
You teased my cock
From the narrow opening in my shorts
Like an indolent eel
And I excused my clumsy fingers
Up your floating dress
Caressing silken juices
Into an amateur artwork

A couple of young team
Patrolling the perimeter
Armed with cool summer ciders
Startled us, as we angled bodies
To hide our arousals
They swigged from crisp cans
Ripe with condensation
And pretended not to have seen

When they had left we began again
Bold enough to feel unencumbered
You exposed me to the rich, warm air
Looking around for voyeurs
I settled into the perfection
Of the moment
Your hand wrapped around me
In the wild Scottish sun
That famous stadium growing tumescent
Throbbing before me
Like a temple

I didn't notice
'Til after we had finished
That we were sat on the edge
Of a fallen memorial
The name was illegible
But I could taste my cum
Still on your lips

Cock

I always planned to suck a cock
The way people intend to visit Vietnam
For the experience
One off the bucket list
But here I am
Booking another ticket
Beginning to learn the language
A frequent flyer

Unintentionally Hilarious Threesome

It's hard to fit two heads
Between two legs
The sensation of four hands mapping
Two mouths overlapping

Harder still after five pints
And a pill
So put my lolling tongue to use
Feed me extremities til I choke
Sit on my face like an armchair
Because tonight
I'm playing snooker with a rope

Time Well Spent

I consider
While performing the act
Of cunnilingus
Just how much of my life,
Thus far,
Has been spent
Performing the act
Of cunnilingus

Days spent languidly lodging
Between soft thighs
Lapping at the architecture
Of beautifully complex evolution
An orchestra to be played
With the flat of my tongue
The sharp electricity
Flowing through a body
Like a string section
Tuning up

I wonder,
While attempting to stay present,
If this is a good use of time -
To provoke a fleeting peak of pleasure
See it plateau into a soft wave
Of sweeping endorphins
And eventually deposit you back
Into the callous calm of the real world

But in truth,
It's a welcome distraction
From all that fucking writing
And it makes a change
To be quite good
At something

Comment Section

I see
you lonely young
men   reaching out with arms
of irony   smoke signals on
PornHub

Nomenclature for Beginners

I roll the vowels around
The soft organ of my tongue
Play with the phrasing
Taste how they fit
You will be honey, baby, darling
Depending on mood or circumstance
Beautiful and stunning also

My cock is to be preceded by hard or big
Always
For the sake of my ego
This pretence must be maintained
Despite its perilous shapeshifting
From acorn to branch

We'll refer to that as pussy
Sometimes cunt
If setting an intention of dirt
Its anatomical terms lost
To a school biology textbook
The only sex education
I ever had

Commodity

I wonder if market forces
Would tolerate
The sale of this
Dilapidated body

Capture images of angles
To arouse and flatter
Barter for bonuses
On the net's dark corners

Some sicko would pay up
For a private gallery
My art supplemented
And who would I hurt?

But maybe I should hold
One pleasure in this life
Without twisting its guts
Looking for money

ALL THAT
FUCKING SAND

Who Will Remember?

i)

Who will remember?

The freckles on my mother's arm
Soft and multitudinous

Losing a watch to red ash Sahara
A lesson in absent sorrow

A prized bike vanished
Discovering my talent for apoplexy

Anxious Sunday night air
Smoke damaged and vibrating

The vivid pink of her toenails
Bare skin resting on my chest

The warm waves of the sea
Come to take me home

An improvised wine shard weapon
Pulled slowly over flesh

A scarred stage, unwitnessed
The indignity of failure

ii)

Do I remember?

The vivid pink of her toenails
Pulled slowly over flesh

An improvised wine shard weapon
Discovering my talent for apoplexy

A scarred stage, unwitnessed
A lesson in absent sorrow

The warm waves of the sea
Soft and multitudinous

Losing a watch to red ash Sahara
The indignity of failure

A prized bike vanished
Smoke damaged and vibrating

Anxious Sunday night air
Bare skin resting on my chest

The freckles on my mother's arm
Come to take me home

Maryhill Juniors

So rarely is a room trusted
To hold both life and death
In such narrow dimensions
Its rich mahogany frame expanded
From absorbing generations of tears
And years of spilled lager

The moustachioed teams of the past
Look on, unmoved
Supping from oversized silver cups
And studying our grief
With an anthropological gaze
From smoke-stained walls

It's a wake –
This time –
But in an hour it'll be indistinguishable
From last week's raucous christening
Once the ties are off
And neatly folded into jacket pockets
Or wives' handbags

Regardless of occasion
The drinking gets done all the same

A Glaswegian hello and goodbye

Are near-identical
A spirited session
Will welcome you into this world
Or shepherd you out of it

I am handed drinks by uncles
Who dare not hug me
But smuggle their contraband affection
In a bottomless stream of Guinness

Plying us with liquid lubrication
Until we allow ourselves
Our greatest indulgence yet -
Permission to feel

Spectre

Death haunts me like a spectre

That's a good opening line for a poem
But it isn't true
Death is *unbothered*
Decidedly indifferent to the outcome
He works on commission
Not by the hour
A detached delivery driver
Blindly following directions
Descending upon unknown addresses
With no clue as to the content
Of his noxious parcel

So why do I sit in all day
Awaiting a bony finger upon my buzzer?
The text says he'll arrive anytime
Between 80-100
But in this city
He always seems to come early
With a next-day box of cancer
Or a gift-wrapped heart attack

So, I should just go out
Get on with my day/life
Be thankful/grateful
Ignore that aching/anxiety
Cause who knows when

The fucker will turn up

But I can't shake the feeling
That I'll be in the Midas midst
Of *really living*
When he comes knocking
Bearing offerings from the cosmic comedy

I don't want to die of cancer at 42
Last requests proffered to Facebook

I don't want to perish in a plane crash
My solipsistic world view willed into truth

I don't want to be struck down by a brain disease
My grey matter folding like origami

Time dances away
Leads us on a merry jig
The promise of a promise
A slice of meaning before we depart
A legacy of memory
That will last a few measly months
In the minds of our co-workers

The older I get, the more I understand
This body is not built to last
It is a temporary vessel
An occasional beast
Destined to break apart like faulty machinery

It only ever goes one direction

And it cannot be negotiated

I'd like to say it grants us insight
Into the precious nature of life
But I have wasted several hours
Writing this poem

Gaff

After Rumi

Aw these feelings
Keep turnin up at the door
And ye've just got
Tae let them in

It's a skoosh when happiness
Drops by fur a few cans
Or contentment is efter a wee catch up
Less so when the buzzer goes
And grief is shuffling aboot
A big awkward bastard
Oan the front step
But ye cannae be rude
Ye've got te let him in anyway

See, if ye kid on ye're no in
Big light aff, blinds drawn
Like a guiser dodger at Halloween
Ye'll find that aw these feelings
Tend tae linger
Hing aboot like a bad smell
Til you let them in regardless

It's better to greet them
Gee them a cuddle at the door
And invite them aw in fur a gaff
Get acquainted, ask questions
They're aw interesting cunts,

In their ain way
Might as well get tae know them
They'll be coming by often enough

This Cat Is Not Your Mother

A light thud like a dropped towel
or hollow idol was your leitmotif,
a blunt note of arrival.

This house is yours, how could I
deny you? Perfect specimen
of liberated, rogue charm.

Neighbourhood flaneur, your
weary features mapped a binary
- domestic indenture clashing

with your net instinct. That
need for the primal prowl, urban
explorer extraordinaire.

I was looking for a sign.
A reason why you had chosen this
specific overpriced, rented flat.

But the truth was simple opportunism
- my window was open and my bed
was still warm with grief.

I'd made pyjamas my uniform.
Worn them dutifully, daily as a
hospital homage to her final days.

And so when you curled comfort
around me like a matted embrace
there was no other conclusion to reach

- you were my mother, reincarnated.
Come to guide me through the poker-hot
obstacle course of bereavement.

I began to leave the window open
dutifully, daily. Mould
my shapeless life around your visits.

You were a herald from the outside
world, a messenger of goings on
beyond the garden limits.

I told you how much I loved you,
all the extravagant ways I'd die for you
as you slept soundly –

a little ball of peace.
One day, desperate for the relief
of simple serotonin

I dropped the soft tartan
of my caustic costume
and began to masturbate.

The cat, sleeping soundly
atop a wardrobe, awoke
to watch my involuntary spasms

with an impassive glare.
Ashamed, I dabbed the aftermath
from the warm pool of my belly button

and shooed you away.
So that I may wallow in my loss
without the distraction of beauty.

I disappeared, to haunt Paris
for a week in the rain.
Leaving my window locked tight.

When I returned, I opened it
wide to the world and the elements.
A portal of invitation.

But you never re-emerged. Your
velvet fur never again gracing
my unwashed sheets.

Maybe you knew, with
empathic certainty, that I was
beginning to live once more.

Or maybe another home had simply
tempted you, provided that warmth
in my absence.

Months later, I watched you
take a shortcut through the bins.
Childlike, I ran out to greet you.

Coyly you scanned my face,
searching for some recognition
and finding none.

All That Fucking Sand

There's a reason
Time is sand
In all those metaphors
Miniscule grains rescued
From an infinite beach
Only to be imprisoned in an hour glass
And immortalised in a bad tattoo
Invariably accompanied by the text
Tempus Fugit
In Roman lettering

Because we can't hold time
It does,
As has been previously noted,
Slip through our fingers
We fill our pockets with it
On sunny days
On golden beaches
Only for the wind to carry it off
When the weather turns

We live under the dictatorship of time
A lender indifferent to the struggles
Of our linear existence
Despite the inevitability of atrophy
We are mandated
To move only forward
Relentlessly

Unquestioning
Oblivious to all that sand blowing away
Returning home
To someone's bad metaphor

Arrangements

I gulped down bile
like the body of Christ.
Welded to a pew,
I listened as the priest –
his tone groping for modernity –
made huge leaps of logic.
Filling in the QE2 sized gaps
in your anaemic biography.

I couldn't help but see it
as a dress rehearsal,
a detailed diorama of future loss.
A test balloon of grief.
So, I made arrangements
in a lockbox
at the back of my head.
Ready for the day.

No doubt you'll die.
A Catholic, working class,
West of Scotland man's death
- painful and preventable.
The sort that scars a child.

But some debts need to be paid
I think,
as I watch you pirouette black-suited,
gripping the dark wood for balance.
Whisky on your morning breath
as the line forms for communion.

Father's Day in the Multiverse

For Father's Day
I bundled you in the back of a taxi
My arm around your disappearing shoulder
I guided your two-stepping feet
To your white Skoda carriage
And selfishly discharged my responsibility
Onto the put-upon driver
Offering my smile as down payment
Lest any seats are pissed
On the short journey home

Back inside the pub
I force down the oiled remnants
Of a gifted Guinness
And robotically scroll my smartphone
A portal to all possible lives:

Here's the one where we enjoyed lunch
At a city centre chain restaurant
Here's the one where our beaming family
Has purchased you a novelty jumper
(which you are gamely wearing)
Here's the one with a sit-down meal
At the local Indian – your favourite -
Holding cheeky pints aloft for the camera

In none of these lives
Are you an alcoholic
In none of these pictures
Can I ever see my face

Xmas in Gartnavel

We crowded into your tiny room
Like a Glaswegian nativity
In new Primark jumpers
Turkeys to the slaughter

Harry Potter absentmindedly cast spells
From his home in the TV
As we attempted to magic together
An illusion of normalcy

Ignoring the tube in your arm,
The bruising on your wrist,
The pint of whisky on his breath

I wonder if Santa remembers
Room 603, Gartnavel

Fly on Rothko

A fly on a Rothko
captured my eye.
Illicit beast,
dragging my ocular down
a burnt blood scarlet
to meet your spindly gaze.

Do you know?
You have reimagined a masterpiece,
given new meaning
to this portal of colour.
Those bold brushstrokes –
alive with contrivance,
shot through with subversion –
now offset with your presence.
An acidic ant
burning through the page.

No-one knows I'm in London.
Like you, I have been hiding
in plain sight. Camouflaged
against a backdrop of someone else's art.
I entrust you this secret
as you creep perimeter,
circumambulating a rich red.

Maybe if I stare hard enough
I will fall into this well of colour,

re-emerge as an insect.
Spend the rest of my days
buzzing idly,
existing without ego.
I would be happy then
in my Kafkaesque cocoon.

But life is an ever-shifting canvas.
Its material changing
from minute to minute.
We are all floating adrift
in a pool of tangerine hues.
A procession of flies
waiting to land on our work
and challenge our runted interpretation
again.

Though form may contort,
its influence puppeted by
the invisible strings of chance.
Beauty remains beauty,
even through kaleidoscope eyes.

ON LEAVING THE SCENE OF THE CRIME

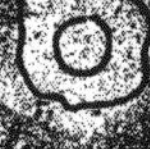

25-34, Separated

We assign the furniture
And apportion the books
Politely
Like two strangers handed a task
An improbable icebreaker
From a team-building weekend
In Carlisle

When you strip away the wallpaper
When the furniture is removed
When the photographs are all in boxes
And the mortgage has been approved

We acknowledge the power
Of each inanimate object
This one here is easy, light
It holds no memories
And is painlessly handled
This one here, however
Requires gloves to grip
Filled to the brim with sentimentality
It is heavy with hopes and dreams
And all the things that will never be realised

Will a warmth still greet me silently?
Will anywhere again feel like home?
When my doubt fills the room like a squatter
When my laughter echoes alone

This is your share of the blame
Your little slice of the failure
To pack away in your suitcase
And take with you
To your next destination
I've swept up all my fault
Hoovered the excess guilt
From under the couch
Filled over ten
Extra strong durable drawstring refuse sacks
Piled high in a mountain of regret
Currently colonising the corner
Of our former bedroom

I'll draw tight my heavy curtains
Attempt to blackout the past
Let this history pass straight through me
Pray this sentence doesn't last

Of course, you can choose
To deposit these artefacts
Donate them to the nearest skip
They are just things after all
But I could orate a history for each one
Write a personal essay on its significance -
Where we were when we bought it
What the weather was like
What dress you were wearing -
These details are seared
Branded on my brain
With a hopeless accuracy
That cannot be binned

So, you clean the surfaces
And I'll hoover the floor
Keys on the counter when you're done
Don't forget to lock the door

On Leaving The Scene Of The Crime

There is no such thing
As the perfect crime
We cannot help but leave
A part of ourselves behind
Microscopic evidence to tie us to the location
DNA that links us to the scene

I am spread all over this house
Careless skin has fallen from me
Congealed into fragments of dust
That lie stealthily
Undisturbed upon bathroom cabinets

My fingerprints are on every surface
Smudged reminders of when we made love
Gripping to tables and armrests
In fevered attempt
To fuse our bodies into one

But I have murdered us
Not in emotional outburst
Or jealous rage
But cold-blooded assassination
Executed from a distance

A shot rings out

Back and to the left

The future stumbles

Back and to the left

Gasps for breath

Back and to the left

Collapses in a heap

You always loved the grizzly details
The latest murder mystery documentary
Or true crime podcast
Sating your desire for the dark penetralia of life
Unbeknownst of your ready-made victimhood

I am the career criminal
Responsible for putting down devotion
Maliciously depriving our passion
The oxygen of time
Rendering the exquisite corpse
Of our near-decade
A macabre inevitability

And now I haunt the crimescene
A ghoul in a joggy suit
The spectre of an ego death
Bony reflection consecrated on the window
Through which we once watched the rain fall
Content in the warm glow of our home
And all we had left to do

They say a murderer
Always returns
To the scene of the crime

This one never left

Season Finale

I squinted
Crumpled my face like the TV pullout
Attempting to see our names flash by
In the carousel of culture
We call the credits

But we weren't there
Not hidden amongst the grips
Or the composers
Or the location crew
Apparently we had not contributed
To the making of this show
Merely been passive spectators
Consuming the feast

And now it's over
Just our reflections staring back at us
From an empty screen
As we contemplate the end

See, when we first started out
You were a modern masterpiece
I binged you
Pored over the nuances of your script
Marvelled at your misc-en-scene

Eight seasons shouldn't finish in silence
Cast and crew moving on to other projects
The writer already hawking a new pilot
I thought the world would shake when we ended
But instead I am asked
What do you want to watch next?

I was invested in this one
Had aligned my life with its transmission time
Mined the wiki for character bios
IMDb for trivia
I even signed up for a forum
Under the guise
ThisIsMyActualFuckingLife123
But my fandom couldn't stop
An eventual drop in broadcast quality

It simply lost its way
The plot meandering
As the writersroom ran out of ideas
Or just went on strike

By the time the later episodes arrived
I'd lost interest
Missing the narrative
Precious turning points ignored
As I scrolled through my phone
Immersed in technicolour updates
Of other people's polished stories

The truth is
That the season finale never really holds up -
Too much pressure
Always an anticlimax
All those loose ends
Tied up in a neat bow

But in real life they drag
Dirtied along the pavement
Get tangled in the masonry of our lives
And when it's time to pull the frayed ends
We risk bringing the whole house down

I built this with you
We wrote this show together
Directed every aspect to suit us
The ultimate passion project
Exec producers of our perfect life

Now its time has come
No longer a ratings darling
Award season in the rear view mirror
Destined to play out as endless mental repeats
In the projectors of our minds
Our own director's cut
Embellishing the truth with imagined detail
The dialogue we wish we'd said
While the cameras were still rolling
While it still made a difference

And I know this is just one
In a litany of lasts
The last hug
The last kiss
The last fuck
Before the credits roll
And all those names
Fade to black

The Extraction

I never loved you
Quite as hard
As that day at the dentist

We arrived like a cold sweat
A trickle of anxiety
Traversing the small of my back
As we occupied the reception
Like a tremulous army

Your name was called
And you bid me farewell
A sailor gone to sea
Leaving me in a tide
Of well-thumbed magazines
And sterile politeness

A half hour passed
In a half dream
Before the door reopened
But you didn't emerge
Like a lukewarm Lazarus
Instead I was beckoned in
To find your frightened soul
Searching for recognition

The gas was a magic
Shrunk you down
Reduced you to a child
Your red eyes greeting me
Even as your lips pouted

You held my hand
Tight like a toddler
Explained how they had
Hurt you
With your silence

My heart deconstructed itself
Formed a Lego kit
Of valves, arteries, aorta
To see you so defenceless
So pure and perfect
And in need of my care

I bundled you like a sick animal
Into the back of a taxi
Still weeping softly
I kissed your forehead
To avoid your cheek
I vowed to protect you forever
That nothing bad would ever befall
Your simple grace

Nothing of course
Except me

Stockholm Photograph, 2012

I can see her.
I can see her.
I can see her.
Set against
a river
in the sun.

She is happy. She is content. She is starting to
Believe...

e,
We had w r
a d e e
l e v r h
k e y w

We were about to w a l k some more.

It is a memory of a past
That was supposed to lead
To a future

A FUTURE.
MY FUTURE.
OUR FUTURE.

a future I rejected.

The photograph never caught my

ego

Ego

EGo

EGO

Dwelling just out of the

FRAME

Eggy Bear

You made a teddy bear
From a pair of my old socks
Festooned with little stitches
Of fried eggs
I walked a hole in either sole

I thought it so industrious
Fashioning life from a pair of old socks
We named him Eggy Bear
Laughed creating his tumultuous backstory

When you left, the bear stayed
Watched reproachfully
From a cleared windowsill
His uneven button eyes
Staring into my soul
Telepathically transferring the mantra
No-one will ever love you
This much again

Withered Vines

You're trying to squeeze two lifetimes into one
She said
And she was right, of course
To commit to one thing
Is to let another die
A future that withers on the vine
before I had time to taste the fruit
(Did Sylvia Plath say that?)

One by one
Doors close
Locking us on our path
Without the time to retreat
Reflect, reassess
Knock another existence
Into our fleeting reality

When you are young
All lines are open
The extended network of life
Mapped out in technicolour glory
Awaiting your meandering itinerary

But we inevitably get waylaid
Set up home at a destination
Go off the beaten track
And find ourselves
Without the time necessary to complete
Our epic journey

Decisions must be made:
Will you travel alone
Or with a companion?
Will you take an adventurous route
Or settle for home comforts?
What stops will you prioritise
With your ever-contracting
Time and resources?

I was under the illusion
My journey was in its infancy
Just a few short steps from home
But I look back and see
The remarkable distance covered
Year on miraculous year
And I know I can no longer follow every branch
To its blooming conclusion
I am hemmed in
By the tyranny of time
And now all my bad decisions
Count for double

Shiitake

I cook with mushrooms now
Feel their surfaces undulate
From springy softness
To earthy notes
I let my fingers read their story
In organic braille

I find an excuse to put them in everything
Nowadays
Porcini in my pasta,
Button in my curry
I'm learning their attributes
Curating my fungus
For the correct culinary journey

It's the freshness
That makes it exciting
Breaching a boundary
Without anyone to tell me no:
You always said it was the texture
All rubbery and slimy
Alien growths
Fried up in a pan

But we pay a price and make a trade-off
And no longer will I smell
The industrious entwining of onions and garlic
Sizzle from the next room
No longer will I glibly state that
Something smells good
And no longer will you tell me
It's just onions and garlic

I will never again
Hear about the intrigue of your work day
Who said what to whom
Despite my love of mundane drama
I've freed up precious time
To wank myself into a coma
Instead

You'd be proud of my Spaghetti Bolognese
I put in a little Pesto
And Worcestershire sauce for a kick
But I know you wouldn't try it
Not with all the mushrooms

You cooked more often than not
Me feigning ineptitude
Borne of laziness
(Turns out it was both)
And though I miss
Your intricately prepared meals
I am only five attempts away
From mastering a perfect pasta bake,
I'd say

I'm forever giving something up
Every inch earned
Must be returned elsewhere
And this freedom has cost us ten years
Of laughter
Of dinners
Of photographs –

Us at that pizzeria on our honeymoon
Waiter whispering Italian
Smiling into the flash
Even as it burned our retinas
Yours a plain Margherita
Mushrooms on mine

ACKNOWLEDGEMENTS

This book would not have been possible without the love and support I have received during its creation. As much as these poems may convince you otherwise, I am not the tortured artist type – I am at my best when I feel the warm glow of stability and contentment in my life. Thank you to all that have nurtured those values in me through these tumultuous few years.

With thanks to my friends who always show up – forever cursed with the burden of buying tickets, purchasing books and generally listening to poetry. I see you and I appreciate you. I know being my friend is not always easy, but I hope it is worthwhile.

To my Scribbler's Union family who crashed into my life out of nowhere to become a fixture of joy in my week. My biggest compliment is that I couldn't imagine life without meeting you all now. Thank you for giving me back the love I put in. My ego has been reshaped by my gratification in watching your successes – may there be many more to come.

With love to all my poetry peers who I have shared stages and drinks with up and down the country – you all continue to inspire me. We are a small, decidedly weird, community but I adore our moments of connection – fleeting though they usually are. I have been privileged to watch your art flourish and lucky enough to call many of you my friends.

With eternal thanks to Stu and the team at Verve Press who picked up this collection with an unbridled enthusiasm that made me feel appreciated from the very start of our relationship. Thank you for trusting in my vision for this collection and for providing the support required for it to come into this world just as I'd dreamt.

With thanks to Stephen Morton for his stunning cover and chapter artwork, whose inimitable style I always wanted to have included in this collection before it even had a title.

Love and thanks to my team of brilliant proof-readers Nasim, Richard, Ross and Leigh-Anne.

And finally, to Jenna. Who valiantly weathered a crash course in loving a poet while patiently listening to every half-baked idea and droning complaint. Thank you for being there with me every step of the way. This is what we do it for.

CREDITS

‘In A Dublin Pisser’ first appeared in *Bella Caledonia*, 7th Feb 2021

‘I Hope I Die At An Orgy’ first appeared in *The Speculative Book* 2021

‘The Free Mark Stole My Humanity (And I Want It Fucking Back)’ first appeared in *The Scribbler’s Union* Vol.1

ABOUT VERVE POETRY PRESS

Verve Poetry Press is a quite new and already award-winning press that focused initially on meeting a local need in Birmingham - a need for the vibrant poetry scene here in Brum to find a way to present itself to the poetry world via publication. Co-founded by Stuart Bartholomew and Amerah Saleh, it now publishes poets from all corners of the UK - poets that speak to the city's varied and energetic qualities and will contribute to its many poetic stories.

Added to this is a colourful pamphlet series, many featuring poets who have performed at our sister festival - and a poetry show series which captures the magic of longer poetry performance pieces by festival alumni such as Polarbear, Matt Abbott and Genevieve Carver.

The press has been voted Most Innovative Publisher at the Saboteur Awards, and has won the Publisher's Award for Poetry Pamphlets at the Michael Marks Awards.

Like the festival, we strive to think about poetry in inclusive ways and embrace the multiplicity of approaches towards this glorious art.

www.vervepoetrypress.com
@VervePoetryPres
mail@vervepoetrypress.com